FIRST LIGHT

FIRST LIGHT
POEMS OF LOSS AND LOVE

Lynn Hoggard

LITERARY PRESS
LAMAR UNIVERSITY

ISBN: 978-1-942956-93-8
Library of Congress Control Number: 2021953431
Manufactured in the United States

Lamar University Literary Press
Beaumont, Texas

ACKNOWLEDGMENTS

I am grateful to Ysabel de la Rosa for her informed and insightful editorial advice on the overall collection and for her specific suggestions on a number of these poems. I am also grateful to the editors of the following journals and anthologies for publishing some of the poems in this book.

Bluestem, "In the Garden"
Broad River Review, "Bearing Witness"
Concho River Review, "Les Gisants"
Casa Esperanza Newsletter, "Casa Esperanza"
DASH, "In a Different Register"
descant, "The Perfect Wound"
Glassworks Magazine, "What Dreams May Come"
JASAT, Journal, American Studies Association of Texas, "A Long and Disciplined Surrender,"
    "Homecoming," "Parting at Dawn, A Love Song"
Mad River Review, "Scraping"
Mezzo Cammin, "As You Read These Lines"
Pisgah Review, "The End of the Parade"
Rosebud, "Fusing"
The Manhattanville Review, "Who We Are"
Voices de la Luna, "What Cannot Be Replaced,"
    "Dashing Through the Dark"
Word Fountain, "An Endless Loop," "Love in the
    Desert"

Recent Poetry from LULP

www.Lamar.edu/literarypress

for Jim
in loving memory

CONTENTS

THE DREAM

THE LIVING

THE TURNING WHEEL

THE UNFOLDING

HOPE

THE COMING DARKNESS

NIGHT

LETTING GO

THE DREAM

LOVE IN THE DESERT
—Chihuahua, Mexico

In forty-five minutes, he said, *go outside*
with a camera and take my picture. If no shots
go astray at the nearby shooting range,
I'll be on top of that mountain,
and I'll be waving my arms.

Then my crazy, jogging husband
was on his way as I sat, camera in hand,
in the Chihuahuan Desert, thinking about
roads high and low that we had traveled
and those who venture or who stay behind.

In forty-five minutes I stood ready,
facing a mountain bathed in sun.
Was he standing there? I saw nothing.
But sight sometimes can crystallize:
I squinted, saw a fine thread at the top

      like the filament in a light bulb—
      haphazard, hazy, thin,

almost absent to the eye, just
at the moment an electrical shock
blazes it into light.

Maybe he's waving his arms, I thought,
or maybe not. I snapped the shot
I hold today: a bare-rock mountain
in the desert, its peak ablaze with emptiness—
no: crowned with incandescence.

WHO WE ARE

We're out of sequence.
Across from a pond—
the odd number
that should've been
where the water is.
Friends and postmen get lost
trying to find us. We ourselves
lose track of where we are.

We keep repainting our number
on the curb—111—as if repeating
the same *one* will wedge us
between 110 and 112.

So we look to the blue-gray pond,
rimmed by sunning turtles, where
perpetual ducks web zigzags,
and we say: *That's us.*
That's who we are.

THE PERFECT WOUND

She hasn't suffered enough, the old one said,
listening to a young soprano sing.
Each of the singer's notes, clear and pure,
made listeners smile, nod to one another.
When the singer finished, listeners clapped
their vigorous approval. Then they browsed
their programs, talked about her gown.

But when the artist picked up his guitar
and started playing, almost in a whisper,
"Alhambra Memories," some let their eyes
go vague or drift away, others let tears
brim, caught in a dream of something precious,
something that they once had loved and lost,
something that would never come again.

He carried them to places that appear
when beauty bends attentively to loss
and moves into the heart to ripen there—
home of who we are and what we dream—

union of the perfect with the wound.
Deeper than hurt, more tethered than despair,
sorrow gives us art that soars and bleeds.

THE LIVING

LOVING

Like the moon, I pull you
from deep inside your liquid core

Like the sea, you heave and roll,
undulating in your turning swells

Like whitecaps, we rise,
dancing in moonlight

IN THE GARDEN

Unlike the myth, her life was never easy.
From the start, Eve worked tirelessly
gathering berries and other fruit, leaves,
and plants, digging and cleaning roots,
shivering or sweating through nights and days
in low, dark caves, always on the move,
while Adam battled hungry animals,
foraged for water he carried back in gourds,
or gathered supple foliage they could weave
for cover from the sun and chilly nights.

They were as firmly bonded as two portions
of one being. Sometimes Adam looked
at her as if she were a miracle.
Other times, he looked away or wanted
her to serve him; she did the same to him.

They raised children, aged, survived.
Whatever God they had was in their bones;

their evil, a wayward excess of desire.
Eventually, Eve became the one
to fathom twistings in the human coil, Adam
the one to grasp the coilings of the earth.

LES GISANTS

As if in a rehearsal, each night we two
are laid to rest in darkness, side by side,
eyes closed, hands lying crossed upon our chests,
like medieval *gisants* carved on tombs.

Yet a whimper says you're not of stone,
says you've glimpsed mortality and cringed,
as you go dream-walking into darker
zones, hoping to meet no one.

I touch your hand, its warmth a reassurance
we're in rehearsal still. Your deep and steady
breathing rocks me back to dream. A little
boat, I rise and fall upon its waters.

Not yet, then, not quite yet.
We're in rehearsal still,
saving our grand performance for another
night, not having reached perfection yet.

THE TURNING WHEEL

BEARING WITNESS

He sits reading in the next room,
having done his required exercises
to delay the coming rigor of his muscles.
The medicine has helped: His hand
no longer collapses as he writes;
his speech appears less halting,
his mind more clear,

Clear enough to let him say,
I feel like the ghost of a man,
as the disease has its way with him,
slowly, slowly turning him—
while he shouts and thrashes in his sleep,
trying to escape the inescapable—
into a torture victim in a cell.

He turns to me. All the love
in the world cannot release him
from the coming darkness.
I touch his face, then turn away,

so he does not see me falter
or know my struggle—
this shaking in my hands.

BEFORE YOU READ THESE LINES
—for Denise Levertov

Before you read these lines,

> three young mice dash through snow,
> having gnawed into our garage
> where the birdseed was

Before you read these lines,

> a man sits downstairs,
> folded hands trembling,
> hosting a visit by Parkinson's

Before you read these lines,

> workers at the house across the street
> seal an opening to the sky
> left gaping since the Christmas fire

AN ENDLESS LOOP
—a film in nightmare

In the desert, he lies alone in pain
inside a high cave, no food or water,

his ankle broken. She runs
for help, is trapped, delayed,

almost immolated. She
lies on a hospital bed, burning

in an agony of helplessness.
Time is surely, surely running out.

Her story, never one of rescue, always
of an endless yearning—she

forever trying to hold back a sun
forever disappearing into earth.

DASHING THROUGH THE DARK

Forget the sleigh bells with the songs.
Instead, go dashing through darkness,
through valleys and forests
with cliffs and things with teeth.

Crouch, then leap, grab hold.
Rest in the moon's curving lip
gaze down from its glow,

Not lonely so much as lost
in love and heartache,
in yesterday,
in all that is to come.

WHAT CANNOT BE REPLACED

Bare branches at the window claw the sky,
as if to beg some power for escape
from winter's grip. The rose's petals gape:
This the time when tender things must die.
And though leaves fall, though flowers wilt and lie
crushed to the ground, spring will come to shape
new buds in fresher forms, to lift and drape
the land in so much splendor that we sigh.

But you, my love, my spirit's fragile throne,
might not be here to greet a summer's day.
No likeness can replace your voice's tone,
your lips or eyes. These are yours alone.
Earth cycles on in its familiar way,
as do we all—unless, my heart, you're gone.

The Unfolding

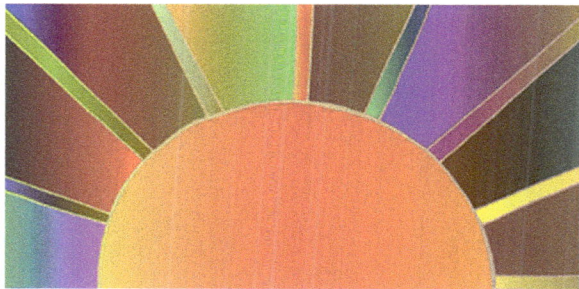

CHRISTMAS MORNING QUARREL

Hurt, anger, self-righteousness
pile around me like kindling.
At their center, I'm tied to a stake,
held in the grip
of a pine tree shorn of tinsel
and all its branches.

Or do I hold the stake?

Let go, let go, let go—
let the holding go,
let the tree, the kindling, go.
Step into the night of my
gut-sickness and bruised heart.
Feel them fold into each other
under the glow of fathomless stars.
Feel them snake their way up my spine.

THE UNKNOWING

Resting on a wall, have you
ever fallen through a doorway
you didn't know was there?

How can you know
an invisible entrance
until you've entered?

Knowledge is like that—
a sudden altering—a trap-door,
a fall from a hot-air balloon.

You happen to turn your head
to see a black chasm
yawning before you.

Revelations
painful
as the soap you rubbed

in your eight-year-old eyes
because you read
soap would make them smart.

What new knowledge
awaits you—
what burning bush?

LOVE AT THE LIMIT

It is only our heartbreak that refutes
all that is ephemeral in love.
—Amor Towles

The ascent into the midnight air,
helicopter blades whirling,
a man supine inside
attacked by his heart,
rises, slips across the moon,
disappears.

A saw severs breastbone,
veins stolen from legs,
four perilous hours of cutting
and stitching together,
a broken offering
lies on the altar of hope.

A lifted hand trembles,
lips move with no sound,
eyes overflow with pain,

mystery, and wonder,
as he seems to ask,
What world is this?

Hope

WHAT DREAMS MAY COME

He lies asleep, holding in his arms
a big, red satin heart like the one
they took out of him
to repair. His legs are sewn up now
where the snaky veins were stolen,
his stomach punctured
for the daily feedings.

Inside him, cells fiercely
trade, fight, and build anew.
He sleeps, but when he wakes,
what future dreams may come
to this carefully mended heart
that holds all that has been
and whatever else may be?

WONDER LAND
—New Mexico Heart Institute

Beds that roll, bend, blink,
swell, and sigh;
dinners that hang from metal trees
and drip from tubes;
O2 pumped through noses;
toilets that droop from beds
in bags.

Armies of people quietly
serving, resurrecting
those in Wonder Land
who now lie supine,
helping them rise and walk
into the world again.

SWALLOWS

I wait for him in the hospital room
while the staff tests his swallow
to see if food enters
his stomach or his lungs.
I swallow my tears.

Outside the sixth-floor window,
swallows wheel in the sunset—
perhaps in some test of their own.

For a moment,
we're all, all
swallows.

CASA ESPERANZA

—support house, Albuquerque, NM

A willow bends low, its leaves
wordlessly tracing a story in the dust,
the message multiple and elusive.

Hope, it says, is sometimes
more vague, more evasive
than despair, than death.

This house, it says, stands
against loss, disease,
and brokenness.

Casa Esperanza, it says, cradles
those in pain and sings
a prayer through their dreams—

of earth's goodness,
of health, of human care,
of going home.

The Coming Darkness

A LONG AND DISCIPLINED SURRENDER

Vowing never to be a housewife,
I studied books past childbearing,
dismissing every invitation
to wear an apron, carry a diaper bag,
remembering up close my mother's rage,
my absent father, the four needy kids—
no choice: wear the yoke, plow the muddy row.

And now it comes around: Caregiver.
Endless days and nights of stress.
Chores without dignity or relief.
Self-denial, sorrow and anger.
When the Fates track you down,
they cleverly deliver what you tried to miss,
a truckload of adult ciapers, an agony of last steps.

> So why dc my arms open in embrace?
> My life, my personal goals, shut down,
> my dreams and joys abandoned.

With tears and tired steps, I serve,
kiss, embrace—finally understanding
love's long and disciplined
surrender.

SHELTERING IN PLACE

It may have been like this
centuries ago in Europe's genteel
outback. A person sequestered herself:
books, walks, hobbies, letters.
She was awash in solitude
and the multi-layered reflections it provided,
meandering the paths of life,
ideas, dreams, the soul.

That sheltered place is now with me
in my country, without the tranquility.
With effort, I convince myself
I'm not in prison. I try to remain
confident that I'll live through
the suffering—maybe even see
our planet's next shuddering
cataclysm.

IN A DIFFERENT REGISTER

He's dying in tablespoons,
I, like most, in teaspoons.
This disease isn't a death knell,
the doctor says, and he's right.
But everything has changed.

A future celebration for us
no longer includes a climb
up Machu Picchu. Now we
celebrate when the bad right leg lifts
from the car and moves onto the pavement.

But we still recall the countless climbs
up our home's stairway, hand in hand,
to the bedroom where we've lain together,
arms around each other, whispering
I love you,
I love you.

PARKINSON'S, YEAR FIVE

Does he feel the giant, claw-tipped fingers
clutch the sides of his head
and squeeze? Does he know
they won't let go until he does?
He fights the growing muscle-lock
throughout his body, even as
the rigor keeps on spreading.
He shouts and thrashes in his sleep
as though caught by a mad animal.
He sweats. His hands are icy. We hug.
He calms, falls back asleep.

Awake, how aware of loss is he?
His stark gaze says he knows,
but he never mentions it, as if
the struggle itself is everything.
That, and gratitude for love,
now falling like small rain
on a drying pond, become a puddle,
where fish struggle, gasping.

55

THE END OF THE PARADE

The celebration passes by.
The band's music—pulsing bass drum,
prancing trumpets, jaunty piccolo pirouettes—
fades like chalk on a rain-washed sidewalk.

For a moment, silence—a held breath.
Then the crowd spills like water,
spreading in all directions.

Finally, only a few kids left,
chasing each other,
and one old woman,
who sits in a folding chair,
with her arms crossing her chest.

She's looking fixedly west
where the sun keeps dropping
step by measured step
into the horizon.

Night

FUSING

This morning I almost took his meds,
so much a part of him,
I felt no border.

Rummaging his brain, I find words
he's looking for
but can't retrieve.

Holding him steady,
I shape his body's other side
as he climbs the stairs.

Confusing, this fusing.

My own body's miseries
and betrayals, hidden
until they ambush.

I ignore them
as I would a growling dog
that follows me.

This cannot end well.
He won't be whole again.
I'll be shattered.

Then once more I'll be confused
when he vanishes inside me,
when I and my rock are one.

IN THE DARK

Hands become trembling claws
unable to button shirts, tie shoes,
write letters (assuming the mind
can sequence order in words).
How much darker
does darkness go?
Does he see past twilight,
the closing lid,
the dark that seals the night?

Today he looks at me,
smiling as I brush his hair,
and says, *I love you*

And, in the dark,
a streak of light
arcs,
        passes on.

LIVING WITH GRIEF

Not everyone is crying as they sweep
the floor of what the two have called a home.
Not everyone is sobbing in a sleep
that doesn't last, as life plays out, alone.
He's gone but he's not gone, yet they're apart.
She speaks but he is absent, though he's there.
She craves the loving eye, the wit, the art
of what they had, not this vacant stare.
He sits inside a room and doesn't cry
for her; instead, he drifts in fantasies
that take him to dark places, make him lie
in hiding from the killers that he sees.
    Not everyone is crying as they sweep,
      just those who love and lose, and, losing, weep.

DRIVING ON EMPTY

Every poem is a momentary stay
against the confusion of the world.
—Robert Frost

The clear, dusty panes
of the bird feeder
say the party's over.
Chaff left from gorging
covers the driveway,
swirling in a fitful wind.

The specialists have all
climbed in their cars
and driven away.
I too am driving away,
leaving my husband
somewhere else, as I
head for distant duties.

Left behind, the feeder
hangs in my mind—

its emptiness, the dusty glass,
the vacant hopelessness
in my husband's eyes.

SCRAPING

Imagine a clam shell—
not a great tool—
just a clam shell.
You're using it
to scrape a surface smooth
on a burn-encrusted metal sheet.
It makes horrific sounds,
like someone hacking up
wads of phlegm.
That noise, you realize,
is your soul.

You keep on—scraping.

SO THIS IS WHO HE WAS

He lies moaning, delirious,
in the hospital bed,
his fever high. Unable to leave
because the rails are up,
he flings his legs at the knees
across them. After a while,
he quietens and starts to hum,
hoarse and off-key,
"Amazing Grace."

Deep in his illness,
he comes full circle,
from resenting faith—rebellious
son of a preacher—to full embrace,
at least in song, as an artist would.
It surges from some taproot—
a place where
rebellion yields, breaks,
bows.

LIMINAL PRELUDE

Snowflakes fall now bigger and faster;
none stay on the ground.

Yesterday he nearly died,
but today he's rallied,
eating and taking his meds.
Temporary, I know.
But that smile—
that flesh—
like no other—
irreplaceable—
even as his shuffling steps
move
slowly
toward the open door.

HOMECOMING

> *And to die is different from what*
> *anyone supposed,*
> *and luckier.*
>> —Walt Whitman

Alone at the dark sea's shore,
he steps into waves that curl
around his toes, caress his feet,
as seagulls overhead wheel and cry.
The water deepens, gently
laving and gathering him,
whispering a husky lullaby,
folding him—his great mother—
into her breast.

He turns, floating in her infinite arms,
lifted by the teeming life below—
scuttling crabs, nesting clams, darting fish,
purple coral hiding in undulating seaweed.
His soul spreads wide

beneath a soaring moon that sings of oneness,
of creation's passion to love and live on,
of the sea's endlessly rocking embrace.

LETTING GO

SAMUEL BARBER'S "ADAGIO FOR STRINGS"

–the tears of things

—Virgil

The composer knew—
when pain and grief engulf,
the notes move slowly,
incrementally,
ascending,
then falling.
They pause,
repeat,
repeat,
repeat,
the way sorrow
follows its dark
circle.

A desperate supplication
swells higher, fiercer,

nearly bursting,
breathless,
unendurable.

Then it falls,
subsides.

Silence.

COFFIN OF THE LEFT BEHIND

Grief is love with no place to go.
—Jamie Anderson

I hold his hand,
the fingertips already cool.
I want to crawl inside
his flesh, hold him
to life from the inside.
I kiss him again and again,
as if kisses can wake him
from this more-than-sleep.

Where can this love go?
I hang my head.

       fragments

               no sense

       darkness

PRESENCE IN ABSENCE

On your dresser lie your keys.
They've been there for two months,
preparing for this moment.
Something must be done with them.
I know the feeling that will come
but know no way to stop it.

I pick them up. Immediately
you are conjured, standing,
keys in hand, studying them,
making sure all are present,
dropping them in your pocket,
walking away.

> Overwhelming—as if
> you had moaned—
> your presence in your absence.
> A lifetime in a set of keys,
> a knife through the heart.

IT COMES TO THIS

The splendor of his beauty
and the horror of his
physical decline
have so spirit-seared me
that I can't move forward.

These past few years,
these memories of his body
hanging on its cross.

THE WAY FORWARD
—for Miki

An icon arrived—a necklace—
a metal engraving of a wax seal,
the image of two trees touching,
separated by a stream.

I finger the trees' forms, think of him
close in the dark night,
the presence of loss cleaving me
at the river of his vanishing.

Is this the way forward?
An image, an icon, a dream?
A bridge to the spirit?
Forever lost, forever with me?

A MEMORY THAT STAYS

Crossing through shadow
as he steps from the exit
of the rehab center, a nurse
on either arm to steady him,
another nurse behind, pulling
a small suitcase, his shuffling step
revealing his fragile health
but his athlete's body, in running
shorts and t-shirt, showing
a vigorous frame, a slight, quizzical
cockiness to the tilt of the head
as he gazes toward the entrance,
then steps into full sunlight
that falls on his hair, his eyes,
his lips, across his cheeks—
lighting a smile
of pure, childlike joy.

PARTING AT DAWN, A LOVE SONG

A rosy-tinted form drifts out to sea
inside the open boat on which you lie:
First light, a glimpse of your eternity.

No Viking rite, despite your ancestry,
no fiery blaze—your glow is soft and dim.
Your rosy-tinted form drifts out to sea.

Eyes closed, you near a future that is free
of all the limits earth has placed on you.
First light now shows us your eternity.

I know your parting wasn't meant to be
a harsh goodbye, your eyes were filled with love.
Your rosy-tinted form drifts out to sea.

I wait and watch, my vigil like a plea
for us to meet again among the stars:
First light, a glimpse of our eternity.

May you enter a reality
outside our orb of blue—go, love, begin—
Your rosy-tinted form drifts out to sea:
First light, a glimpse of your eternity.

James Hoggard (1941-2021) published twenty-three books, including novels, poems, plays, short stories, essays, and translations. He served two terms as president of the Texas Institute of Letters and in 2000 was named Poet Laureate of Texas. He held the Perkins-Prothro Distinguished Chair in English at Midwestern State University in Wichita Falls, Texas, where he taught from 1966 to 2014. He also taught in England, France, Spain, Mexico, and Iraq. A dedicated athlete, he completed nine marathons and more than twenty 100-mile bicycle races. He married Lynn Taylor in 1976. He has two children, Jordan and Bryn.

In May of 2015, Jim was diagnosed with Parkinson's-with-dementia. Four years later he suffered a heart attack, leading to five coronary bypasses. Congestive heart failure, COPD, and four bouts of aspiration-pneumonia followed. He contracted Covid-19 and died on February 23, 2021.

84